ECHOES *of* SILENCE

ECHOES *of* SILENCE

Awakening the Meditative Spirit

Robert Rabbin

InnerDirections PUBLISHING

InnerDirections Publishing

INNER DIRECTIONS FOUNDATION
P.O. Box 130070
Carlsbad, California 92013
Phone: (800) 545-9118, (760) 599-4075
www.InnerDirections.org

First Edition
Printed in Canada

ISBN: 1-878019-09-0

Book & cover design by Joan Greenblatt

Library of Congress Catalog Card Number: 00-130215

IN APPRECIATION

This book is dedicated to Leah Grillo, a five-year-old goddess from Montana who showed me what love is all about. A blown kiss, a tap on her heart—"You are in here," she whispered. I will never be the same. May she have a joyous and prosperous life.

With further acknowledgements to:
Sri Nityananda, Swami Muktananda, Nisargadatta Maharaj, Ramana Maharshi, Jean Klein, J. Krishnamurti, Jelaluddin Rumi—for their ruthless clarity and inspiration.

Also:
Sandy Faith—finally, her own special line;
East Coast Carol Ann—for her enthusiasm and support beyond the call of duty;
Avram Davis—for his generous Foreword, and almost three decades of eccentric friendship;
Matthew and Joan Greenblatt—my personal Light brigade, as in "here comes the cavalry" to save the day;

And all my lovely friends whose loud voices helped bring this book into form.

CONTENTS

The publisher gratefully acknowledges
the kind help of *The Ward Foundation*,
Box 2137, Friday Harbor, WA 98250
in sponsoring the publication of this book

FOREWORD   There are only a few questions in our life worth asking, such as "Who am I?" "Who is this one that breathes and speaks, hopes and fears?" "Is it possible for me to be happy?" "What is reality?" As we seek answers, we discover the summit of truth is difficult to attain. With mounting urgency we press on, but difficulties persist because the questions exist within the mind which, by itself, is ill-equipped to answer them. Eventually, our quest leads to teachers who can inspire us to find answers beyond the mind and guide us to reach the summit of inner truth. As a guide, Robert is one of the best. He is always telling us a story and, as Muriel Rukeyser said, "The Universe is made of stories, not atoms."

Most spiritual teachers use words differently from the rest of us, whether it is the sonorous melody of chanted *sutras* or the dream-time language of the Torah, the God intoxication of Rumi or the ironies of Chuang Tzu. The great teachers seek to bend language to the needs of the instant. They recognize that language is mere smoke and mirrors pointing to a higher reality—the reality of the One. Because language is the medium the mind understands, good teachers make use of it as they would make use of any sturdy tool—but they do not mistake the tool for the intended result. The way we best learn to break through the constraint of language is to use words in such a way that they are deconstructed, even as they are uttered. Through image and logic, through inner music and subtle insight, through apparent paradox and metaphor, the teacher uses words to go beyond words, as Robert does when he writes:

> *Meditation is a soundless sonic boom*
> *in the silence of the stopped universe.*

Robert's *sutras* reflect a deep reality—the place of Being itself. Though the journey to this primal place is sometimes harrowing, it is also playful, for the universe is really a dance of poetry and song. In truth, those who take this "journey of essential questions" are from the first step held and caressed by a profoundly deep understanding, aptly reflected in this book:

The heart of meditation is eternity without center or edge,
pure lovers braided and blended by other lovers
we can never meet.

Robert writes in such a way that readers/listeners can have their heart opened in one moment. Bam! Just like that. His every word serves to bring us into the heart of the moment, which is silent and wordless. Only in this way and in this place can life's essential questions be answered. Robert teaches through his being and encourages us to enter our own being and drink from our essential nature. He understands that meditation is far more than just sitting, counting breath. Meditation is the ultimate feast of the soul, a drunken shout of freedom. As he writes:

Meditation is a feast wholly unto itself,
with you and I centerpieces on its handcrafted table.

Echoes of Silence is a rich harvest. All who eat at its table will be delighted and will benefit from the wisdom of this book.

—Avram Davis, Ph.D.
Founder and Co-director of Chochmat HaLev meditation center
Author, *The Way of Flame* and *Judaic Mysticism*
Editor, *Meditation from the Heart of Judaism*

PREAMBLE

All wisdom is in the Self. Know your own secret. Know your own Self.

SRI NITYANANDA

The divine principle which creates and sustains this world pulsates within us as our own Self.

SWAMI MUKTANANDA

You need nothing except to be what you are.

NISARGADATTA MAHARAJ

Meditation is our real nature now.

RAMANA MAHARSHI

But yet it was empty: a vast boundless emptiness which nothing could ever fill, transform, or cover up. Meditation was the ecstasy of this emptiness.

J. KRISHNAMURTI

When the ego is abandoned, there is only silent awareness, total presence.

JEAN KLEIN

Here's the new rule: Break the wineglass, and fall toward the Glassblower's breath.

JELALUDDIN RUMI

PREFACE This book is a collection of *sutras*—aphoristic depth charges, terse statements lobbed into the psyche where they silently explode and cause all conventional knowledge to implode, leaving a quaking-pulsing-shimmering aftermath of uncontrollable freedom and spontaneity.

Freedom and spontaneity characterize the mystery of existence—distilled into essence—which we are, through and through, from top to bottom, inside and out. In this book, I name the freedom and spontaneity of the mystery of existence *meditation*.

Meditation is commonly thought to be a practice or method, rooted in some mystical/spiritual/religious tradition or philosophy, whose purpose is to disabuse us of delusional notions about the nature of self and reality. Meditation is likewise defined as a path to enlightenment or self-realization, a set of steadying training wheels that helps us to ride the bike of our innate essence—to pedal our way towards the inherent clarity, wisdom, and compassion of our true nature. Meditation thus implies a means of becoming, an action or process that leads from here to there, a catalyst that produces an effect not already in evidence. Even if one believes that meditation is the expression of our inner being, the intimation of becoming is still there, the implication that we must do something special to become or demonstrate what we are.

I don't particularly dispute this notion of meditation, but I have noticed that almost all of us, while claiming we want to go to heaven, don't want to die. In other words, we don't want to trade the traveling for the arriving, the doing for the being, the future promise for the present Reality. As long as we are traveling, doing, and believing exotic promises, our separate self can persist. Our egocentricity is a cockroach: it's almost impossible to get rid of it. We will find some way to subvert the supposed means of radical and irreversible transformation—meditation—into another game of our egoistic foolery.

I think there is a better way around the tireless sentries of our self-centered thinking and living. I have, as perhaps you have, experienced a spontaneous awakening into a life out of time, place, and category. In this awakening, one finds oneself solidly on the summit of awesome, selfless living, a summit unreachable, because it is already reached, unattainable, because it is already attained. This is meditation, this standing on the already-conquered summit of superb views and immaculate air. To say it this way is to click our heels together and wake up in Kansas, where we have been all along. No traveling, no becoming, no awakening is really necessary.

In this book, meditation does not refer to a practice, technique, or path; it does not refer to a means; it does not refer to an imagined end or idealized state of consciousness. It does not imply even a trillionth of a millimeter of movement from here to there.

In this book, meditation means the purest distillation of the creative power of the universe in whose uterus unimaginable conceptions occur and collide outside of time or place. Meditation refers to the incontrovertible fact of existence whose whole measure can only be taken by itself.

That existence is what we are. That existence is the only existence there is.

Meditation is a freedom for which no practice can prepare us. Meditation is an impenetrable mystery, beyond understanding because it is not an object and cannot be known as one. Meditation is the very fact of life, so immense that only silence can approach.

The silence that can approach meditation is the trumpet blast and rolling snare drum signaling our entry into the heaven we have never left.

SUTRAS

GLORY

Meditation is not a means to realize our desires,
to become more effective, or to develop psychic abilities.

Meditation is not a means to anything.

It is the end of all such becoming
as our simple-minded flesh and bones could want.

When we reach this end that is meditation, a new life begins.

It is not our life,
not the life we used to name with our name
and carry around like a trophy of rare achievement,
but life itself, flashing through what used to be us.

Meditation is life without name,
without form.

Meditation comes first
and last.

Meditation bookends all becoming
with its fiery finality.

We can't understand this;
we can only burn the trophy case

and then live gloriously in the new life that is meditation.

L O V

The heart
of meditation is
eternity without
center or edge

ERS

Grammatically, to meditate is a verb.
Realistically, this is not true:
meditation is not a verb.

Verbs imply time.
Meditation is timeless.

Verbs imply doing.
Meditation transcends doing.

Verbs imply becoming.
Meditation *is*.

Verbs are conjugated.
Meditation is undivided, unchanged, all-embracing.

The heart of meditation is
eternity without center or edge,
pure lovers braided and blended
by other lovers we can never meet.

AWAKENING

Concentration is a useful skill,
a manipulation of attention and energy.
Concentration helps us realize our desires,
become more effective, and develop latent capacities.

Meditation is not a useful skill
and it doesn't help us the way concentration does.

Concentration is to meditation
as a pilot light is to the sun, as a droplet is to the ocean.

Meditation means to be transcendently awake.

When we are this wide awake,
the little world disappears
in the same way sleep does
when the alarm clock goes off.

When the little world disappears,
the ocean, the sun, and the wide-awake world
come into clear focus.

Meditation means to be so wide awake
that nothing need ever be said.

MEDITATION
MEANS TO BE
SO WIDE AWAKE
THAT NOTHING
NEED EVER
BE SAID.

PRIDE

CONCENTRATION YIELDS fruit with enough
juicy kick to make us proud.

Concentrating for weeks, months, even years at a time,
we achieve insight and have revelations about existence.
Our aura brightens.
We look through the back window and see the past,
through the front door to the embryonic future.

But these achievements have a crummy halo
which ruins everything:
Pride.

It can't be helped.
If we do something, *we* do it.

That inescapable ownership
is the crummy halo
which ruins everything.

Meditation cannot be practiced,
so it can't ever swell
the pride-gland of practitioners.

Within meditation, all is too quiet
for doers of something and their halos
of achievement.

Within meditation,
there are no successes and wretched failures,
no powerful kicks, no pretenders to the throne.

There is only the one silent prince,
the braided lovers,
the measure unto itself.

TECHNIQUES

There is no "how" to meditation.
It isn't something we do.
It is what we are,
underneath the skin, meat, and seeds
of the guava-body.

All techniques require
effort,
intention,
discipline,
will.

The incantatory means of mantra,
the practice of postures and control of breath,
sweeping the mind's porch
and scrubbing cells clean of clutter—
these are techniques of concentration, not meditation.

Concentration wears a watch and knows
when to start and when to stop.
Concentration owns a ruler
to measure progress.

Meditation has neither watch nor ruler.
Meditation never begins and never ends.

Meditation is a feast wholly unto itself,
with you and I centerpieces on its handcrafted table.

HUMILITY

There are no meditation masters,
because no one can master meditation.
If you hear of a meditation master,
keep your money in your pocket.

If you don't believe this, go ahead, make the effort
to master meditation yourself.

Only don't do it half-heartedly.
Make a supreme effort:
resolve to master meditation
as a grid of steel within a slab of concrete.

One day, your soul will hoist a white flag
on your behalf.
You will know what this means.

Your soul will throw the white flag of your effort
into the abyss of false mastery
where it will flutter downward
into the deep gorge and settle silently over boulders
strewn with thousands of other flags.

Then turn toward the soul of greater knowing
and offer yourself

as a servant to a master—
and become the servant of meditation.

We must become servants of meditation
so meditation will become our master

and show us what real life is all about.

WE MUST BECOME
SERVANTS OF
MEDITATION

DUAL

Many people know about meditation, and talk about it nonstop.
For many, meditation is a movie—"Oh, yeah, I saw it."

Intellectualizing about meditation is
as useless as a raincoat in a typhoon.

We can't "know" about meditation,
just as we can't "practice" meditation.
If we know and practice, it isn't meditation.

All knowledge is based on knower and known,
subject and object.
This is duality.

Duality is a useful way of understanding the world we live in,
it's how we know to not step in front of a bus.

I T Y

Duality, however, is a fatal error
when it comes time to be what we are.
Duality is to meditation as an umbrella is to the falling sky.

Within meditation there is no subject, no object.
Within meditation, the knower, known, and knowing
of common days and nights does not exist.

Meditation means to look left, and see right.
Meditation is an equation
in which mirror and image have equal value.

Within the typhoon of meditation, there is no subject, no object:
no raincoat, no rain, no wind, no blown-apart buildings.
Within meditation, there is nothing else, or other.

Somehow, we've got to get used to this fact
as the essential fact of life.

I am worlds within worlds,

mystery upon mystery,

love beyond love.

REASON

A sage once said,
"Reasoning and reason keep you far from it."
It refers to meditation.

Why did the sage say that?
Because he meant it, that's why.
Meditation is not reasonable.

Reason isn't even a blip on the screen
of meditation's radar.

Meditation does not comfort
the cardsharps, swindlers, and con men
who tell us to live safe little lives
and not rock the boat.

The boat needs to be rocked.

Meditation says,
I am worlds within worlds,
mystery upon mystery,
love beyond love.

Meditation is what we are
after everything we think we are
hits the ground with the suddenness
of a hammer knocked from a bench.

What is the point of being reasonable about it?

Meditation is as reasonable as a three-legged Cyclops.

There is no free lunch.
Everything has a price,
including meditation.
People who say meditation should be free
don't know what they're talking about.

Meditation is expensive, very expensive.
It costs more than most people are willing to pay,
which is why concentration is more popular—it costs less.
Of course, we get what we pay for.

The price of meditation is our life.
There is no getting around this.
In order to meditate, to know meditation,
to be absorbed into and by meditation,

we must die to everything we think and know,
everything we were and hope to be, everything we imagine and believe.

We must die.

And then comes the resurrection, so sublime, so vivid, so true . . .

RESURRECTION

SILENCE

SILENCE is exquisite.
In the world of words,
meditation and silence are synonymous.

They refer to an emptiness
in which what we are stands alone.

What is this emptiness?
It contains only what we are, nothing else.

When silence bites us like the snake it is,
we forget everything.

The snake's potent poison
spreads through our body
and slithers up the spinal stem—
when it enters the shivering brain
everything dissolves

except the silent truth, which appears before us,
behind us, above us, within us—
what is true suddenly stands alone.

We know this emptiness when we are in love,
not "in love" as an infatuation,
but in love

as a lone traveler walking without bags
in the dark desert-silence of meditation.

Of course, emptiness is a trick word.
But so is meditation, and so is silence.

In the real world of non-words,
silence and meditation are skyscraping lovers
with arching granite foyers.

STRATEGIES

A lot of teachers talk about spiritual strategies
for getting everything we want.

They don't know what they're talking about.
It's materialism in a costume.

Too many teachers talk too much
and too many students listen too much.

Meditation doesn't promise anything.
It isn't a strategy.
It simply *is*.

When we exist within meditation,
there is no room for strategies of becoming,
achieving, attaining, owning.

Within meditation,
silence is the only strategy,
because everything is too sudden for planning,
too rich to want,
too hushed for noise.

Meditation doesn't

promise anything.

It isn't a strategy.

It simply IS.

THINKING

What is the purpose of all our
THINKING
THINKING
THINKING?

How much thinking do we really need to do?
Even a dog will quit chasing the bone,
sooner or later,

but when do we ever quit chasing
the bone of our thoughts
thrown first here and then there
by the dead brain?

Running back and forth
is a game for faithful dogs
who know when to quit.

We ought to play the game
of the living brain,
the one with sensual centers
of intuition
and jazz riffs till dawn.

Meditation is the living brain's romp:
an indoor/outdoor, all-weather game

in which nothing moves
and no one wins

but fireworks explode each
evening at 6:00 p.m. sharp

and every train leaves and arrives
on time, to the second.

A SAGE said if we still have an interest in outcomes,
realization isn't for us.
He might have said "meditation,"
because meditation is the living realization of our essence.

Either we want essence, or outcomes.
We can't have both.

Even if we think we can, argue we can, prove we can—
we can't.

Meditation is that essence of life in which all wanting
and hoped-for outcomes
have returned home

to the embrace of loved ones long missed,
almost forgotten.

That homecoming is a real festival
of fullness, food, and drunkenness,
drinking cups, glasses, and goblets
full of reunion wine.

Truly, this is hard to imagine;
we have wanted so long
we've forgotten how it all started—

how we left home to prove some point.
Now we've returned.

Meditation is this wild homecoming
where outcome meets essence
and understands who is right.

ESSENCE

ATTACH

MENT

We don't like thieves who take what we love,
or think we love.

We're so used to loving our attachments
we naturally confuse one with the other.

Do we really love our stereo, that painting, this necklace?
Maybe we're only attached to them—
the canes and crutches of bad habits we're afraid of losing.

Love is different from a bad habit,
as different as wheat is from the chaff.

Meditation is a daring thief who sneaks into our house
when we're asleep or on vacation

and steals our chaff, robs us blind—
but fills our cupboards with golden wheat.

When we wake up or return
to find everything gone
but the wheat of that thief
whose signature is love—

hell, burn the house down
because you won't need it anymore.

Meditation has harvested our heart
and taken the bounty to market.

CONTROL

THE RAREST GEM on Earth
is a person who has stopped meddling
with moon cycles and migratory patterns.
These people are one in a billion.

A perfect symmetry already exists.
Who said we should be the world's jackboot police force?
Clubbing and crushing innocent heads,
we are way too determined to be
the central meaning of the universe.

It's possible for the same thief
who takes the heirlooms
of our attachments
to steal our desire for control.

Pray for this thief to find you.

And then, only then,
will we know what living is.

Real living is love, not control.

Meditation is the final surrender of
mutant militias who want to master

what is not theirs to master.

SAFETY

Comfort, safety, and security are appealing, but dangerous.
They are false harbors which protect only tiny ships.

Once we are safe, we don't want anything to rock our boat.

After we have clearly marked the boundaries
of our comfort, safety, and security,
we build fortifications on those marks.

The walls go up, the sentries are posted, the watch begins.

What do we watch for?
Anything outside that wants to come inside.
This is what we fear.

Living safely within fortifications,
fearing what is outside, loading our guns—
what kind of life is this?

Meditation dissolves false boundaries,
and transforms fear into love.

Meditation is the true harbor of such insane safety
that no tiny ships can weather its storm.

MEDITATION IS
A FOOTPRINT IN WATER,
A HANDPRINT IN AIR.

ACTION

Action from thought is loud,
brutish, and self-centered.
It rushes wildly from one thing to the next, without care.
It leaves piles of paper, packaging, and other debris.
Someone always has to clean up the mess.

Action from meditation is clean, silent, and deep.
Meditative action does not go from one thing to another.
It is, and then it isn't.

Meditative action is deft and echoless.
Nothing is left behind.
There is no mess.

It is rounder than a circle,
a footprint in water,
a handprint in air.

MEANING

Whenever you assert something—anything—ask yourself,
"What do I mean?"

Having said whatever you say next,
again ask yourself, "What do I mean?"
And again.
And again.

Continue to challenge yourself in this way
until every explanation, justification, opinion, belief,
and defense of self falls before the question,

"What do I mean?"

Finally, you will have no answer to your self-questioning,
and you will admit that you do not know what you mean,
that everything you say and believe
is robotic, conditioned, and obsolete
before the last word is out the door.

You will be silent.
You will remain silent.

That silence is meditation,
the heart of wisdom,
the center of the universe.

HOLINESS

It's easy to mistake a spiritual appearance for a spiritual person.
We are trained like circus bears to believe
a pope's brocade, a rabbi's shawl, a swami's yogic postures,
a dervish's starched gown, a shaman's bag of amulets,

all indicate something important.

Maybe they do, and maybe they don't.
Whether people who dress in certain ways
are truly spiritual people is an open question.

It may be that their holiness is our imagination.

We ought to be more concerned about
whether our own soul spits meditative juice
through the holes in our body.

Holy people ooze silence through
every pore of their body.

Only those people whose holes ooze meditation
can truly be called spiritual.

The others are merely dolls, scarecrows, and mannequins.

MYSTERY

WHAT DO YOU SEE WHEN
YOU LOOK AT THE WORLD?

What do you see when you look at the world?
Do you see that sycamore tree?
Or the bougainvillea?
Do you see a mound of sugar-dusted almonds?
Do you see a slaughterhouse, hospital, or airport?

Do you see a wide-open marketplace, ready for plundering?

Do you see good and evil, right and wrong, spiritual and worldly?

Keep looking.
Keep looking until you see the mystery,
until the mystery sees you.

When you are eyeball-to-eyeball with the mystery,
when neither blinks nor turns away,
when only the mystery is,

that is meditation.

HAPPINESS

DON'T WORRY about your own happiness.
Don't pursue it. Leave it alone.
Forget about it.
It isn't important.

"I'm happy" is as big a boor as "I'm sad" or "I'm frustrated"
or "I'm lonely" or "I'm afraid" or "I'm confused."

Don't let boors live in your mind, in your heart, in your soul.
Kick them out.

What is important?
That's what we should find out.

Meditation.
That is important.
What you are is important.
Your happiness is not.

Happiness comes and goes according to moods
and circumstance, according to what we have
and what we hope to get.

Meditation doesn't come and it doesn't go.
Meditation does not depend upon anything.

EXCITEMENT

Excitement is a poor man's soul experience.
Adrenaline rushes are not life force surges.

Hormones and chemicals produce effects,
but those effects are tiny—actually, they are pathetic.

When a galaxy of stars leans one way and then another,
as though drunkenly reeling from left to right
banging its shoulder from wall-to-wall down the corridor
of your own house,

well, that effect is huge.

That effect is meditation.

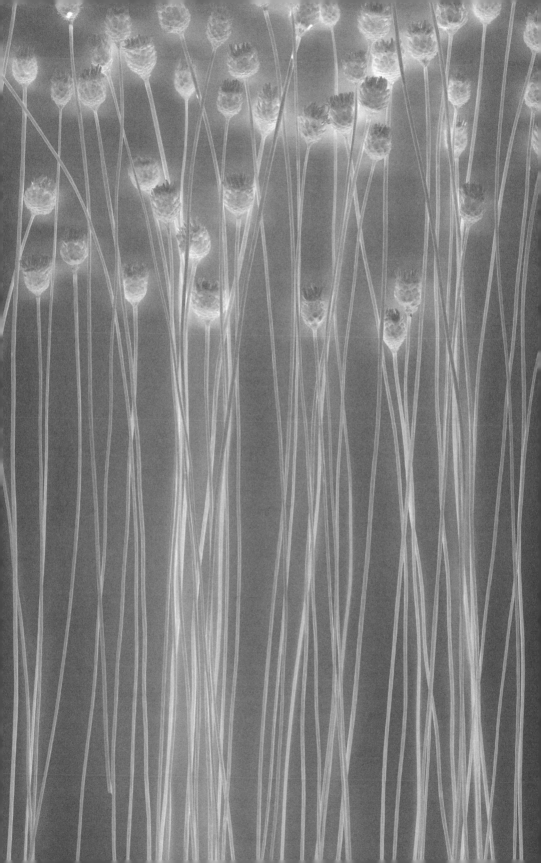

DESIRE

The world wants us to stay hungry
so we'll habitually buy things
that do us no real good,
like Park Place in a Monopoly game.

The world's blunder teaches us
that we can only fill the big hole in our gut
by owning everything in creation.
And that is supposed to be the game of life.

Isn't it true that our whole life is one big shopping spree?
Have we ever stopped wanting things, even for a minute?

Stop believing the world, because the hungry hole
in your gut will never be filled
no matter how much you eat and own.

It's true our gut is empty, but only because
we listen to the world: that listening is the hole.

Instead, listen to your fullness.
Where is it?
There, there, and there.

Your fullness is everywhere
you stop wanting.

Not-wanting is meditation.

Meditation has no room for fake desires
because it is already full, overflowingly full.

Meditation is a full gut of food
the world has never tasted.

SERVICE

WHEN WE KNOW what we are
we offer the peace of saints.

We transmute old wrecks into new cars.

We do this without effort,
intention, or self-consciousness,
because healing and renewal is the
very fingerprint of meditation.

We are a constant grace to broken hearts
although we don't know how we do it, or that we do.

It is what we are.

Meditation touches pain and fear
with an alchemical hand,
brightening lost souls to their original luster.

Look, this arm is golden.
Look, this leg is golden,
this face, this head, this heart—

all golden.

Meditation is the golden alchemy
that transforms pebbles to pears,
and pears to perfection.

INVISIBILITY

THE VISIBLE WORLD is a facade,
a puritanical curtain that hides from our eyes
the outlandish lovemaking of gods and goddesses.

Their invisible world is where the heat begins
and grows into our visible world as afterglow.

Without beauty, what is awe?

Without silence, what is wonder?

Without love, what is the heart?

Without the invisible world, what is the visible?

Meditation carries us across
the threshold of the invisible world,
into the bedroom of erotic delights.

BELIEF

We do not like the mystery to cast shadows
on our linear gods.

Once we believe something,
we want it to stay that way.

We don't want anyone to revise
the taut and tidy scriptures
that tell us what to think and what to say.

If we can explain, we think we are knowledgeable.
If we can justify, we think we are right.
If we can rationalize, we think we are moral.
If we can defend, we think we are heroic.

Meditation won't stand for this nonsense.

There are no linear gods in the mystery of meditation.

TRUTH

I tie my shoelaces before I go out,
because I don't want to trip.
I change my car oil every three thousand miles.
I am careful when I balance my checkbook.
My dishes are as clean as polished stone.

Some of my friends laugh
because my socks are laid side-by-side
in the drawer according to color.

You could say I like to have all my ducks in a tidy row.

But no amount of cleaning, organizing, or labeling
will help us to know what we are.
What we are cannot be marked and stored like winter clothes.

We want to organize what we are—
label it with black marker and then
store it in tiny bins and drawers, stack it on shelves and racks.

Meditation cuts through all of this.

Meditation is an unexpected earthquake
that shakes our ordered existence
into a thousand directions

and leaves our neat home a total wreck.

Setting record

MEDITATION

after record,

IS THAT

breaking the tape

LIGHT FASTER

in the same instant

THAN LIFE

the starter gun is fired.

DEFINITIVENESS

Everyone wants definite answers.
Everyone wants to know who, what, when, where, how—
as though life means getting an A+ in journalism class.

The problem is that today's precision
is tomorrow's confusion:
life is a speed demon who runs
faster than any of our definite answers.

If the room I enter is dark,
I turn on the light.
I don't sit down and cry,
hoping someone will take me by the hand.

I want light,
not a hand sneaking around in the dark
promising it knows the way.

Meditation is that light faster than life,
a track star who sets record after record,
breaking the tape in the same instant
the starter gun is fired.

Meditation is here, crouching,
and there, arms thrown back,
at the same time.

Meditation is a speeding light
too fast for definite answers.

SPONTANEITY

I shop with a list I put together
before I leave for the store.
Walking up and down the aisles,
I put just what I need in my cart.

Living is different from shopping.

If we make a living list
and carry that around with us,
we'll miss life.
We'll only notice the corn flakes,
bananas, and bagels on our list.

Life jumps out at us. It doesn't stay put,
like bottles of catsup
standing steadfast in place as we stroll by.

Life is always hopping around,
ambushing us with humor and ambiguity.

We don't have time to look at our lists
of how to live if we are really living.
Ready or not, here it comes.

Meditation is life unrehearsed and unrefined,
falling on us from the inside and from the outside,
out of order, nothing where we want it to be,
no signs to tell us what is in aisle number one, two, or three.

There are no aisles in real living, no lists, nothing packaged.

Real living is raw, organic—stupendous.

ORIGINALITY

I like to say and know what I've never said or known before.
I don't try to do this, it just sometimes happens.
When it does, a voice from somewhere says,
"Now *you* are alive!"

I don't know if the voice is speaking to me or to someone else.

When I hear people speak of what the Buddha said,
or what Jesus said, or what anyone said,

I feel less alive

than when someone just throws me a left hook
from the same place Buddha, Jesus, and all the others
threw their left hooks.

I'd rather be slugged in the face with originality
than pleasantly massaged
with what has already been said
and known by someone else, in another time.

Originality is the voice from somewhere that says,
"Now *you* are alive!"

Meditation is this originality,
this slugfest of life without precedent,
brawling and loving *now*, not before, not after.

KNOW

LEDGE

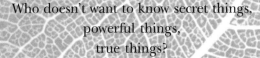

Who doesn't want to know secret things,
powerful things,
true things?

That's why we turn to scientists and priests and politicians,
because they tell us things we want to know and believe.

But their clever words do not reveal
the truly powerful secret
we most want to know:

When love breaks our bones and splays our heart
what further knowledge do we need?

Isn't there something within us, already formed
that knows what we want to know; all the secrets?

Why do we listen to false oracles for the answers we already have?
Why do we practice this self-deception?

Meditation is the oracle that breaks our bones
and rends our heart
with the secret too heavy to hold

with only one body.

The eye-camera,

MEDITATION

the seeing,

IS THE

the technicolor vision—

GORGEOUS

all together,

MOMENT

this is meditation.

CLINGING

Our minds are very grabby.
Even when a sage tells us "Don't grab,"
we grab that.

If the aperture of our eye-camera opens wide
and we see something fantastic, gorgeous,
we have to take a picture. We can't let it go by.

We have hundreds of albums made of these pictures.
We grab and collect, grab and collect.
The old albums are stored in the shed
while the new ones are put on the coffee table.

Meditation does not grab or collect.
Meditation is not afraid the gorgeous moments
won't come again.

Meditation is the gorgeous moment,
the eye-camera, the seeing, the technicolor vision—
all together, this is meditation.

PRIORITIES

We want some things we can't afford.
Other things we can afford,
but aren't sure if we want to pay the price.

We can all afford meditation,
in spite of the fact that we say
we can't.

We can.

Meditation's price is simply the conceit
that we are the center of the universe.

We aren't.

We should pay.

What do we get?
Storms of surprise
and adventures beyond our control.

Which would you rather have:
a vanity case of busted dreams

or roller coasters and rock 'n' roll?

Decide for yourself.

NOT-KN

Some people think the highest knowledge means
to have it all figured out.
This is not so.

The highest knowing is not-knowing.

Some people think not-knowing is ignorance.
This is not so.

Ignorance is thinking we know
what is unknowable.

When we lose our footing and slip
on the slick pavement of our vanity,

OWING

we fall into the unknowable
ditch of meditation.

The ditch of meditation is deep and wide:
full of freedom and miracles,
it cannot be filled.

We cannot measure the ditch of meditation,
we cannot pour foundations for knowing—

we can only trip into its not-knowing
and laugh at the scholars
scampering for more footing.

WILLFULNESS

Anger is a symptom of willfulness.

Willfulness is a hard and nasty felon
who lurks inside us with loaded guns.

My way or the highway.

We can't sentence our felons of willfulness
to prison terms, they can't be dealt with that easily.

In the meantime,
they create all kinds of
murder and mayhem,
sorrow and sadness.

Why?

What is so special about the way we want things to go?

Meditation is a different kind of living
in which our hardened will
snaps its neck
in the vise of emptiness.

Another way opens before us,
soft and kind, not hard and nasty—

a knotted muscle somehow stretching
from our relaxing body to the edge of our essence.

REALITY

What do we mean when we say the real world? Do we mean the world we can see, taste, touch, and smell? Do we mean the world of our hunger and ambitions? Do we mean the world of our imagination?

Do we mean the world of our ideas and images,
of our hopes and wishes, of our disappointments
and missed opportunities and broken hearts,
of our joys and pains, our victories and defeats?

If any of these were the real world
they would never disappear.

But they do.

As they disappear, the real world of meditation appears,
stepping forward in tuxedo and expensive shoes,

the master of ceremonies
for entertainments that never end.

THE BARNACLES THAT ATTACH to rocks and hulls of ships
do not easily release their grip.
One by one, they gather and attach
gather and attach
until rock and hull are invisible, forgotten.

Barnacles also gather within us and attach
to our otherwise gleaming hulls.

They are different from the crustaceans that
weight and bury rocks and ship hulls,
though their shells and grip are every bit as hard and firm.

The barnacles that gather and attach to our hulls
include thoughts, beliefs, and emotions;
experiences of pleasure and pain;
memories and expectations.
Too many to name and classify.

Like rocks and ship hulls, we seem content,
even willing, to let these barnacles gather and attach.

We should not be so willing.

If we want the hull of our ships to gleam,
we must pry these barnacles off, not one by one,
there are too many, but all in a single stroke.

Meditation is that single stroke.

Meditation is our gleaming hull
cleaned of barnacles, as bright as hand-rubbed steel.

CONDITIONING

LISTENING

MEDITATION IS WHAT
LISTENS
TO OUR LISTENING.

We can't practice meditation,
but we can practice listening,
which is different from hearing.

Hearing is when the mallet of sound simply
hits the soft skin of our inner drum.
We hear thousands of thumps and thuds every day.
Hearing is not artful, but automatic.
Listening is artful: it occurs when the mallet of sound
strikes in between our inattention, our thoughts and
beliefs, our anger, judgement—even our agreement.

Listening is pure, unfiltered.
Listening is opening to the here and now.
We cannot listen if our mind is in last Tuesday
or next April, if the sounds are blended with
the discordant music of our fantasies.
We cannot listen if we are ready to respond.

Listening is simple, empty and open,
without pretense or posture.
We listen when we are struck by the meaning,
by the essence, of each thing as it is.

Each thing is first formed by its sound,
its vibration. To hear this subtle form
of each thing's sound before it appears as a leaf
or a truck is to listen.
Listening is a good practice.

Meditation is what *listens* to our listening.

PRACTICE

SPIRITUAL PRACTICE is a wrecking ball,
a huge swinging fist that smashes
the joists and studs of delusional homes.

Spiritual practice destroys the apartments, condos
and houses of conceptual thinking.

Conceptual thinking is a security system against reality.
Spiritual practice disarms those belief systems,
throws open the front door and proclaims,
"Reality is welcome here!"

Conceptual thinking invents the pictures, vases, coffee tables,
carpets and couches that fill our minds.
Spiritual practice throws everything out
and keeps the old clutter from coming back.

Spiritual practice keeps our homes clear
and our minds freshly painted with emptiness.
Spiritual practice drapes our hearts
with reality.

If you want to know what reality is,
turn off the security system, throw everything out
and let the front door remain open.

Then, one Friday night, with real dinner guests
seated and laughing around a real table
eating a real meal and drinking real wine

meditation will enter
as another kind of wrecking ball
and blast everyone from reality to kingdom come.

POSTURE

Meditation is that

MEDITATION

posture in which

IS

all the vertebrae of

A DIFFERENT

creatures like cosmos,

KIND OF

eternity, infinity, and

POSTURE

love are stunningly aligned.

All spiritual practice is a matter of posture.
If we are leaning too far to the left,
we have to be corrected towards the right.
If we are leaning too far to the right,
we have to be corrected towards the left.

If we are too materialistic, spiritual practice
will lead us into the subtle realms of creation—
opening our eyes and arms to embrace delicate nuances of being.
What was one-dimensional will become multidimensional.

If we are too convinced of our own dogma, spiritual practice
will take us into ambiguity, paradox, parallel universes,
and all manner of confounding realities.

If our hands won't let go of what we want
spiritual practice will knock our knuckles.
If we are too proud, spiritual practice will cut off
our legs just above the knees.

If we are too silent, we will be made to speak.
If we are too weak, we will be made strong.
If we are too humble, we will be made great.
If we are too mean-spirited, we will be made kind.
If we are too violent, we will be made peaceful.

Meditation is a different kind of posture,
a posture in which no straightening can occur.
Meditation is that posture in which
all the vertebrae of creatures like cosmos, eternity,
infinity, and love are stunningly aligned;

standing together, shoulder to shoulder, heads high,
backs perfectly straight, there is not a lean in the bunch.

ANXIETY

Anxiety is a preview of coming attractions
or a review of past attractions
revived for another showing.
Anxiety certainly has nothing to do with what's happening
today, now, right this minute.

When we watch the coming or past attractions of anxiety,
we won't see a circus tent ten feet in front of us.
We'll fall like a drunk through the tent flaps, bump into a clown,
knock over a young girl eating cotton candy, or get trampled by elephants.

Anxiety is so blinding a storyteller that we get
trampled by elephants
in the tent of our own mind.

In meditation, there are no previews of coming attractions.
In meditation, there are no reviews of past attractions.
In meditation, there are no blind drunks getting trampled by elephants.

Meditation is a circus in which the high wire acrobats
of here and now tumble, roll, and turn in space,
lifting themselves higher and higher,
not falling, not ever falling down
towards the always empty net.

My best friend never leaves me alone.
I can't do anything, go anywhere, or see anyone
without my best friend tagging along,
like a shadow with its own body.

You'd think enough would be enough, but it never is.
My best friend loves me and won't leave me alone.

I'm getting used to this, but I'd like to have some time alone.
My friend says he can't trust me. He's right.
I'd probably forget him, and do all the stupid things
that I hardly ever do when he's around.

He has a powerful effect on me.
Like a conscience with a hand mirror,
my friend is always showing me
what I'd rather not see or take into account.
He makes me a better person, in spite of myself.
Isn't that what best friends do?

My best friend is death, death is my best friend.
This shadow with its own body who follows me everywhere
reminds me that each minute is the full life span,
and that each thing we do is waiting for us at the next corner.
Without death, I start thinking I've got forever,
and I can hide from my actions. I don't, and I can't.
My best friend shows me how to see my next step with hindsight.

Death is my best friend in the same way
meditation is death's best friend.
Meditation is death's shadow with its own body.
Meditation teaches death about that life
which never begins, and never ends.

If we let death tag along during our life,
we will learn what meditation knows
about life without death.

DEATH

ILLUSION

Sleight-of-hand artists deceive us in two ways:
they make us see what isn't true,
thus preparing us to not see what is true.

Whipping the walnut half-shells from left to right,
they smile and ask, *Where is the pea?*
There!
Wrong!
There?
Nope.
There?
Wrong again.

Twenty dollars lighter, we go home, grumbling,
having seen what isn't true
and not having seen what is true.

These magicians are everywhere,
whispering in our ears from cradle to grave.
They mold our minds with made-up stories
then shout down our inner knowing
with marching bands and uniforms,
with scepters, medals, and money.

They rule the world and the world rules us.

We always lose to these rogues,
and when we run out of cash
we start hocking bits and pieces of our soul
until one day we are bankrupt
outside and in.

Meditation is the wise old witch
who laughs at the world's rule,
that sleight of hand which makes us
see so often what isn't true
that we can scarcely see what is.

EGO

We are bullies with an unnatural brain
who think if we don't intimidate events
and outcomes into existence
nothing will happen.

The rest of nature knows that existence
does just fine by itself.

Existence impregnates itself with what comes next.
We are nature's only bullies,
kicking and punching at life,
bruising it black and blue.

Why do we do this?
Perhaps it's because our unnatural brain flashes desperate
images of loss and death, of pain and suffering—
exhorting us to kick the groin and punch the serene face of life
in some kind of misguided survival instinct.

We are not the origin of events and outcomes:
they begin from farther away than dead stars
still shouting their brightness for all the world to see,
billions and billions of years after they have perished.

Meditation is this distant place which remembers everything,
even each leaf, each stone, each next step for you and I.

Meditation has no feet or hands with which to
kick and punch the rest of creation.

MEDITATION
HAS NO
FEET OR HANDS
WITH WHICH
TO KICK AND PUNCH
THE REST
OF CREATION.

SHAKTI

Plants and trees are fed by streams of sap
flowing from stem to leaf, from trunk to branch.

There is another kind of nourishing sap,
an invincible current which lights
the interior corridors of the living world.

From salamanders to cormorants,
from coral reefs to collapsing stars,
everything has this secret current circulating
through its body,
breathing life into each vital part.

Without this current, nothing can live.
Without this current, nothing can exist.

Meditation is the heart
that pumps this sap-current
into the special arteries
that crisscross the bodies
of all living things.

SELF-INQUIRY

We are always hungry with questions,
and when we ask a question, we expect an answer.
If we don't like the answer, we may ignore it,
ask another question, or look elsewhere for a better answer.

Our questions demand satisfaction.
Once satisfied, we will rest for a while—
as after eating a big meal—until we get hungry again.
Then we'll ask another question.

We are binge-eating questioners who demand answers.

There is one question which has its own hunger.
That question cannot be answered,
because any answer will not satisfy its hunger.
Even if you can answer and feel full
this question will not.

Who am I?

This is the question with its own hunger.
Go ahead, answer. Are you full? Are you satisfied?
Ask it again.
And again.

Keep asking this question,
while asking the question's hunger if it is satisfied.

The hunger of Who am I? will never be full
until it is fed with meditation.

Meditation is not an answer we might want,
but it is the answer this question wants.

Meditation is the meal that cannot be eaten
because its fulfillment is final.

SOURCE

*Meditation is a soundless
sonic boom in the silence
of the stopped universe.*

Stop signs do not joke.
Neither do cops.
We have to come to a complete stop,
or we'll get a ticket.
No rolling stops, no almost stops,
no stop and goes.

Stop means stop.

Silence is like a stop sign
for more than cars and trucks.
It is for the whole universe.

Silence is the whole universe
completely stopped, unmoving,
dead still, no pins dropping,
no cells breathing,
no synapse firing.

This silence makes a tomb's silence sound
like a jackhammer.

Meditation is more silent still—
more silent than silence—
because its stop is final.

Meditation remains stopped even
after the universe starts up again.

Meditation is a soundless sonic boom
in the silence of the stopped universe.

LOVE

Love with conditions is not love

Love and unconditional love
are not two different teams playing
for some championship in late January.

The problem is with our language:
love is unconditional.
We don't say "wet water."

Love with conditions is not love;
it is something else and needs another word.

Just as love does not exist within conditions,
meditation does not exist
within a person whose body
is not split open by the spiritual ax.

ECSTASY

Not all alcoholics love just bottled spirits.

Some alcoholics roam the boozy bars of the ecstatic soul,
drinking themselves deaf and dumb,
sitting for days and years on stools
in stuporous silence, dead drunk,
staring into space from the far greater space
of their own drunkenness.

What's wrong with that?

Go ahead, get drunk—

I mean really drunk—

and then run through the streets yelling,
"Hey, everyone, I'm drunk.
Quick, come here and kiss me!"

Meditation is a never-ending bender
in the red-light district of pure soul,
where men and women get as drunk as they want
without pretense or remorse.

Now, let's take *those* spirits back to the guilty world
and get them drunk too, on the real stuff.

Meditation is the real stuff served in the bars
of your own soul, and it's free.

Go ahead, get drunk!

PHOTO CREDITS

Jane English: page 30

Matthew Greenblatt: page 31

Pan Brian Paine: pages 72-73

John Loewenstein: pages 78-79

ABOUT THE AUTHOR Robert Rabbin has had a lifelong interest in the true nature of self and reality. In 1969, he began to research mystic traditions while practicing meditation and self-inquiry. In 1973, Robert trekked overland to India where he met Swami Muktananda, with whom he studied for the next ten years.

Since 1985, Robert has been facilitating self-inquiry seminars, designing executive and corporate retreats, and serving as an advisor to leaders of a broad range of companies and organizations.

For additional information and to contact Robert,
please visit his website at: www.robrabbin.com.

INNERDIRECTIONS PUBLISHING is the imprint of the Inner Directions Foundation—a nonprofit, educational organization dedicated to exploring authentic pathways to awakening to one's essential nature, in the spirit of Self-inquiry.

Our activities include publication of the highly acclaimed *Inner Directions Journal* and a distinctive selection of book, video and audio titles that reflect clear and direct approaches to realizing *That* which is eternal and infinite within us.

These publications reflect the nondualistic "ground" from which religions and spiritual traditions arise—the Infinite Consciousness that lies at the Heart of all.

To request information or a free catalog of publications call, write or e-mail:

INNER DIRECTIONS
P.O. Box 130070
Carlsbad, CA 92013

Tel: (760) 599-4075
Fax: (760) 599-4076
Orders: (800) 545-9118

E-mail: mail@InnerDirections.org
Website: www.InnerDirections.org